A LifeGuide®

D0289355

THE KINGDOM OF GOD

10 STUDIES FOR INDIVIDUALS OR GROUPS

Greg Jao

With Notes for Leaders

IVP Connect
An imprint of InterVarsity Press
Downers Grove, Illinois

InterVarsity Press
P.O. Box 1400, Downers Grove, Il. 60515-1426
World Wide Web: www.ivpress.com
E-mail: email@ivpress.com

InterVarsity Press® is the book-publishing division of InterVarsity Christian Fellowship/USA®, a student movement active on campus at hundreds of universities, colleges and schools of nursing in the United States of America, and a member movement of the International Fellowship of Evangelical Students. For information about local and regional activities, write Public Relations Dept., InterVarsity Christian Fellowship/USA, 6400 Schroeder Rd., P.O. Box 7895, Madison, WI 53707-7895, or visit the IVCF website at <www.intervarsity.org>.

LifeGuide® is a registered trademark of InterVarsity Christian Fellowship.

All Scripture quotations, unless otherwise indicated, are taken from the Holy Bible, New International Version®. NIV®. Copyright ©1973, 1978, 1984 by International Bible Society. Used by permission of Zondervan Publishing House. All rights reserved.

Cover image: Bill Hatcher/National Geographic Image Collection

ISBN 978-0-8308-3099-2

Printed in the United States of America ∞

P	20	19	18	17	16	15	14	13	12	11	10	9	8	7
Y	21	20	19	18	17	16	15	14	13	12	11	10			

Contents

Getting the Most Out of
The Kingdom of God

It's a simple quiz that both Christians and non-Christians frequently fail: *What did Jesus most often teach about?* Whether I ask the question in smoky campus coffee shops, in well-appointed offices or in brightly painted Sunday school rooms, I hear similar responses: Love. Forgiveness. Repentance. Holiness. How to have a relationship with God. Freedom. I rarely, if ever, hear the correct answer—the kingdom of God.

What is the kingdom of God? It's neither a place (like the kingdom of Saudi Arabia), nor a people (like the church), nor a distant future state of being (like heaven)—although it can include any of these things. Rather, it refers primarily to the expression of God's sovereign, active rule and only secondarily to the infinite realm over which he reigns. As a colleague describes it, "The kingdom of God is *about the dynamic of God's Kingship being applied.*"[*]

It's also a theme that stretches from Genesis to Revelation and integrates the Bible's sixty-six books into a unified storyline:

> In the beginning, a king creates a realm of delightful diversity and unsurpassed harmony. Reflecting his love and trust, he entrusts his two primary stewards with the development of his realm under his overall rule. Unfortunately, a disgraced former government minister encourages the stewards to rebel against the king's rule, casting the entire realm into disarray, decay and disease. The stewards (and their numerous descendants) then establish their own alternative, petty kingdoms. Time after time, the king sends emissaries to invite them to end their insurrec-

---

[*]Allen Wakabayashi, *Kingdom Come* (Downers Grove, Ill.: InterVarsity Press, 2003).

tion and to accept a treaty which acknowledges his rightful rule. And, time after time, the rebels agree—but they inevitably renege and continue their rebellion. Under their inept and corrupt governance, the realm's diversities become divisive and its harmonies fade into a half-recalled melody which lingers only in the memories of a few.

Grieving and angered, the king undertakes an unusual campaign of reconquest: he infiltrates the rebel lands and announces that he is reestablishing his reign. Wherever he travels, he defeats the rebel forces with provocative demonstrations of love and justice. He restores harmony and wholeness. He triumphs in the decisive battle, not by an overwhelming show of force but by offering reconciliation to the rebel forces through a surprising demonstration of humility and self-sacrifice.

Shocked into sensibility, some rebels repent of their rebellion and enlist in the king's program for reconciliation and reconquest. Asserting the king's rule over rebel-held territory, they slowly begin to construct new harmonies from the diversities and to nurture order from amidst the disorder. They confidently labor in light of the king's inevitable triumph.

Other rebels, however, ignore the king's victory. But they have become aware of rumors that the king plans to complete the mopping-up operation rather forcefully.[*]

Though not every biblical author mentions "the kingdom of God," their worldview assumes its eternal reality, present activity and eventual and inevitable victory in every relationship, location, culture or system which denies God's reign and rule. The Old Testament authors, living in anticipation of this victory, wrote as if God's reign would break into creation in a single, decisive moment. The New Testament authors, observing Jesus' life, death and resurrection, discovered that God came in and through Jesus to establish his kingdom. They came to realize that while Jesus inaugurated the kingdom at his first advent, he would complete the conquest only at his second. And

[*]Graeme Goldsworthy, *According to Plan: The Unfolding Revelation of God in the Bible* (Downers Grove, Ill.: InterVarsity Press, 1991).

until he returns, the kingdom of God would come through his followers' Spirit-empowered witness in both word and deed.

Both sets of authors confidently asserted that God's program of installing the kingdom would bring justice to the oppressed, salvation to the lost, community to the alienated, reconciliation to the rebellious and complete peace to creation. It would mark the restoration of the abundant life humanity was created for—absolute communion with God, one another and the world in which we were set. It would imprint God's character and will into every sphere of human endeavor: spiritual and physical, intellectual and emotional, cultural and social. It would result in the Spirit-inspired worship of God through Christ.

In this LifeGuide we will explore the nature of God's reign and how Jesus inaugurates and embodies the kingdom's program of renewal and restoration in his life and ministry. We'll discover the personal, social and cosmic theaters of operation in God's campaign of reconciliation. And finally, we'll investigate what it means to live in the time in-between the initial invasion and the completion of the campaign.

God's two-stage program confronts humanity with clear imperatives: repent, worship, reorient your priorities and pursuits, and participate in the renewal of creation. May we hear and respond.

Suggestions for Individual Study

1. As you begin each study, pray that God will speak to you through his Word.

2. Read the introduction to the study and respond to the personal reflection question or exercise. This is designed to help you focus on God and on the theme of the study.

3. Each study deals with a particular passage—so that you can delve into the author's meaning in that context. Read and reread the passage to be studied. The questions are written using the language of the New International Version, so you may wish to use that version of the Bible. The New Revised Standard Version is also recommended.

4. This is an inductive Bible study, designed to help you discover for yourself what Scripture is saying. The study includes three types of questions. *Observation* questions ask about the basic facts: who, what, when, where and how. *Interpretation* questions delve into the meaning of the passage. *Application* questions help you discover the implications of the text for growing in Christ. These three keys unlock the treasures of Scripture.

Write your answers to the questions in the spaces provided or in a personal journal. Writing can bring clarity and deeper understanding of yourself and of God's Word.

5. It might be good to have a Bible dictionary handy. Use it to look up any unfamiliar words, names or places.

6. Use the prayer suggestion to guide you in thanking God for what you have learned and to pray about the applications that have come to mind.

7. You may want to go on to the suggestion under "Now or Later," or you may want to use that idea for your next study.

Suggestions for Members of a Group Study

1. Come to the study prepared. Follow the suggestions for individual study mentioned above. You will find that careful preparation will greatly enrich your time spent in group discussion.

2. Be willing to participate in the discussion. The leader of your group will not be lecturing. Instead, he or she will be encouraging the members of the group to discuss what they have learned. The leader will be asking the questions that are found in this guide.

3. Stick to the topic being discussed. Your answers should be based on the verses which are the focus of the discussion and not on outside authorities such as commentaries or speakers. These studies focus on a particular passage of Scripture. Only rarely should you refer to other portions of the Bible. This allows for everyone to participate in in-depth study on equal ground.

4. Be sensitive to the other members of the group. Listen attentively when they describe what they have learned. You may be surprised by their insights! Each question assumes a variety of answers. Many questions do not have "right" answers, particularly questions that aim at meaning or application. Instead the questions push us to explore the passage more thoroughly.

When possible, link what you say to the comments of others. Also, be affirming whenever you can. This will encourage some of the more hesitant members of the group to participate.

5. Be careful not to dominate the discussion. We are sometimes so eager to express our thoughts that we leave too little opportunity for others to respond. By all means participate! But allow others to also.

6. Expect God to teach you through the passage being discussed and through the other members of the group. Pray that you will have an enjoyable and profitable time together, but also that as a result of the study you will find ways that you can take action individually and/or as a group.

7. Remember that anything said in the group is considered confidential and should not be discussed outside the group unless specific permission is given to do so.

8. If you are the group leader, you will find additional suggestions at the back of the guide.

1

The Character of the King

"Who's in charge around here?" When the world seems disordered or the future uncertain, we instinctively look for strong leaders—individuals with trustworthy character, wise action and unimpeachable integrity. These kinds of leaders inspire our confidence, our trust and our dedication to make things right.

GROUP DISCUSSION. Describe the character or activities of a national or world leader—past or present—whom you admire. What does your choice reveal about your values?

PERSONAL REFLECTION. Identify a personal situation or world event that feels out of control. Then write down some characteristics of God that you want to keep in mind, and incorporate those characteristics into a prayer about the situation that concerns you.

When one leader sincerely praises another, it's high praise indeed. In this study, we'll learn the many reasons David, the king of Israel, finds to praise God, the King of kings. *Read Psalm 145.*

1. Looking throughout the psalm, who all does David assert will worship God the king?

2. David praises God in verses 1-7. How does one of these qualities inspire you to worship?

3. How do prior generations influence David to respond to this knowledge of God's qualities (vv. 5-7)?

Describe a situation when someone influenced you to respond to God in a similar way.

4. What do you learn about the character of the King and of his kingdom in verses 8-13?

5. God's kingdom refers not to a location but to the experience of living under his rule. Where do you see some of these characteristics of God's kingdom reflected in your community?

6. What specific actions could your church or fellowship take to manifest these characteristics more obviously in your community?

7. Compare (a) the creatures and people listed in verses 13-20 and (b) the way God acts toward them. (You may want to create a chart to summarize this information.)

8. What do you learn about God's agenda as king?

9. Imagine what it would be like if your country fully shared God's agenda. Describe how the choices it would make might be different.

10. Describe one specific way you could reflect God's agenda at your workplace or in your neighborhood this week.

11. What particular aspects of God's attributes and actions described in this psalm do you celebrate (v. 21)?

Ask God for courage to further his agenda and to reflect his character in your home, neighborhood and workplace.

Now or Later

Begin to keep a list of places where you see God's kingdom agenda and character positively expressed in the world. Use the news, the Internet, and your interaction with friends and neighbors as your primary sources. Review this list when you finish the studies in this guide.

2

The Kingdom's Coming

Mark 1:14-45

First impressions matter. That's why leaders craft their inaugural speeches and choose their first acts in office carefully. Their first words and deeds set the pattern and tone for the rest of their term in office.

When Jesus bursts onto the public scene, he begins with a surprising announcement: "The kingdom of God is near. Repent and believe the good news!" (Mark 1:15).

GROUP DISCUSSION. Recall the first time you met the other people in the group. What were your first impressions of each other?

PERSONAL REFLECTION. What are your earliest impressions about Jesus? How has your understanding of Jesus been enriched since then?

Our first impressions of Jesus involve both word and deed. *Read Mark 1:14-45.*

1. What does Jesus' first public message communicate about the character of his ministry (vv. 14-15)?

2. How does Jesus demonstrate the authority of the kingdom of God in verses 16-20?

3. How might the relatives and employees of the early disciples have felt about their decisions?

4. What benefits do the other people of Capernaum experience as the kingdom of God arrives in Jesus (vv. 21-34)?

How could God use you to demonstrate that the kingdom of God is also good news to your community?

5. Describe the potentially competing power structures in Capernaum that the arrival of the kingdom of God challenges.

Which of these power structures seems most resistant to the challenge of the kingdom of God today? Explain.

---

6. How could God use your fellowship or church to challenge these competing power structures?

---

7. What do Jesus' actions in verses 35-39 reveal about the kingdom's priorities and values?

---

8. Describe a time when prayer and quiet enabled you to re-order your life around Jesus' kingdom priorities and values.

---

9. Lepers were religiously unclean, physically ill, socially excluded and emotionally distanced from the community. How does Jesus authoritatively offer full reconciliation to the leper in verses 39-45?

10. Who is negatively affected by the leper's subsequent disobedience to Jesus' authority?

Which groups of people are most often affected by your disobedience to Christ's commands?

Spend some time praying for boldness to show the good news of the kingdom to specific people and situations where God is giving you an opportunity.

Now or Later

Read Luke 4:14-30, which gives an expanded version of Jesus' earliest teaching. How does the quotation from Isaiah help explain the physical and spiritual changes brought by the kingdom of God?

Definitions of "parable" "metaphor"

3

"good soil"

What is

An Offer *the Kingdom* You Can't Ignore *My Response*

Matthew 13:1-45

46

"the seed" (nurtured by the good soil)

When I first started writing for my high school newspaper, the veterans offered rookies like me important guidance: show, don't tell. Powerful writing invites readers to experience a story rather than merely read the facts. Jesus used parables for the same reasons: to allow readers to experience the truths he taught.

GROUP DISCUSSION. What stories did your parents enjoy telling you as a child? What do you think they hoped you would learn from them?

PERSONAL REFLECTION. What story or song has changed the way you think about the world? How did it do so?

5 teaching sections, like the Torah

In the central teaching section of Matthew, Jesus uses a series of stories to show what the kingdom of God is like. *Read Matthew 13:1-45.*

1. Retell the parable of the sower using a new metaphor instead of farming (vv. 1-9).

in general

2. What actions and attitudes ˄characterize those who receive the secret of the kingdom from those who do not (vv. 10-17)?

ignore the offer

my   *in particular*

How do your attitudes and actions ˄compare with those who receive the secret of the kingdom?

3. Draw a chart which compares (a) the type of soil, (b) the response to the message of the kingdom the soil represents and (c) an example that you have seen of this kind of response (vv. 18-23).

4. Jews in Jesus' time expected the kingdom of God to come all at once and to immediately inaugurate a dramatically different world. How does the next parable correct these misconceptions (vv. 24-30)?

5. How would the parables in verses 31-35 encourage disciples discouraged by the prior parable?

6. Mustard plants spread quickly, covering entire hillsides with plants between four and fifteen feet tall. Yeast naturally spreads throughout a lump of dough, changing its texture and consistency. How have you seen evidence of the inevitable growth and pervasive infiltration of the kingdom of God in the systems of the world?

7. Compare the parable of the weeds (vv. 24-30) with Jesus' explanation of the parable (vv. 36-43). When and how do the differences between the children of the kingdom and the children of the evil one become obvious?

8. How and why does the master choose to deal with the wheat and weeds?

9. How does the parable shape your attitude toward evil in the world?

10. How do the parables of the weeds, mustard seed and yeast encourage you to be both realistic and hopeful?

11. Retell the next two parables using images from your own life (vv. 44-45).

12. What qualities and choices would mark the life of someone who was willing to give up everything to pursue the kingdom?

How is your life similar or different?

Spend some time praying that God's people would be faithful in understanding, obeying and pursuing his kingdom values.

Now or Later

Flip through your local newspaper. Where do you see signs of the kingdom advancing? being challenged? Pray that God's kingdom would come and his will would be done in each of those events.

4

Mission Statement for a Kingdom

A good mission statement focuses successful people and organizations toward a clearly-defined goal. It aligns their aspirations, directs their activities, defines their success and casts a vision for the common future. It controls who they are and who they will become.

GROUP DISCUSSION. Describe your proudest achievement. What makes it so important to you? What does it reveal about your values?

PERSONAL REFLECTION. If you could choose only five words to describe your personal mission in life, what would they be? Why?

The stories we tell about our heroes (whether in fiction, politics, business or church life) reflect our values. The stories told to us by our heroes shape our values. *Read Matthew 20:1-28.*

1. How are the stories told by Jesus similar to and different from the stories told by your heroes?

2. Which of the characters in the parable do you most identify with (vv. 1-15)?

3. What does the landowner's character reveal about the values of the kingdom of heaven?

4. Describe an opportunity you have had to demonstrate these kingdom values and characteristics in your community, workplace or school.

How would those places change if Christians more frequently acted like the landowner?

5. Compare the future Jesus predicts with the future anticipated by the mother of Zebedee's sons (vv. 17-23).

6. How should Jesus' description of his death have changed her understanding of the kingdom's values?

7. How do you reflect this understanding of the kingdom's values and characteristics in your vocational and economic choices?

What practical choices could you make this week to better reflect the kingdom's values and characteristics?

8. Jesus does not discourage his disciples from seeking greatness. How does Jesus refocus their definition of greatness (vv. 24-28)?

9. Describe a person you know who models a pursuit of greatness through service.

10. What everyday choices would someone committed to pursuing Jesus' path to greatness face?

What choices do you face this week as you pursue Jesus' path to greatness?

What choices does your church or fellowship face this year as you pursue Jesus' path to greatness together?

Ask God for the wisdom to identify places where you could live out kingdom values more completely and for the courage to do so.

Now or Later

The next two stories in Matthew illustrate how Jesus lived out the values he taught. *Read Matthew 20:29—21:11.*

11. How does Jesus reinforce his teachings to the disciples as he interacts with the two blind men (20:29-34)?

12. Jesus enters Jerusalem as a king. Retell the story as if he were entering a political capital today (Matthew 21:1-11).

How would his entry differ from the inaugural events associated with most modern political leaders?

13. How does the way he enters Jerusalem reflect his teachings in chapter 20?

14. Reflect on the kingdom values Jesus taught and demonstrated. How would the church be different if it more faithfully reflected these values in its actions and attitudes?

How would the world be different?

5

Kingdom in Words and Deeds

Acts 8:4-25

"Oh the places you'll go." It's more than the title of a book; it's a description of life as I have lived life in light of God's kingdom. I have gone to different countries, moved into new careers and entered into challenging relationships. And no matter how daunting or painful the situation, God has met me there in surprising and, ultimately, delightful ways.

GROUP DISCUSSION. Describe a situation when cultural, ethnic or racial differences distanced you from someone else.

PERSONAL REFLECTION. Recall a time when God brought you into a situation that frightened you. How did he equip and encourage you to act faithfully?

After dramatic growth in the first seven chapters of Acts, the church experienced persecution, and the Jerusalem-based disciples were scattered throughout Judea and Samaria. The ethnic hatred between the Jews and the Samaritans was intense and mutual, and their history together was filled with violence. *Read Acts 8:4-25.*

1. What prejudices and fears might Philip have faced as he traveled into Samaria (vv. 4-5)?

2. What groups of people raise similar prejudices or fears in you?

3. Philip went to proclaim Christ. How has your commitment to proclaim the good news of the kingdom of God forced you to confront prejudice and fear in yourself or in others?

4. Identify the content of Philip's message and the characteristics of his ministry (vv. 5-12).

5. How do his deeds illustrate the truth of his words?

6. If your church or fellowship were to confront similar prejudice and fear for Jesus' sake, what specific deeds might best illustrate the gospel truth of your words?

7. Contrast the words and deeds of Simon prior to his conversion (vv. 9-11) and Philip during his stay in Samaria (vv. 12-13).

Compare the response of the Samaritans to each man.

8. Consider the response your words and deeds evoke among your friends and neighbors. What is one change you could make to your words and deeds to become more like Philip?

9. How does God affirm to the mostly Jewish believers in Jerusalem that his kingdom includes the historically despised and religiously unclean Samaritans (vv. 14-17, 25)?

10. Does your experience of the kingdom of God include people who are separated from you because of history or culture? Why or why not?

11. Review the entire passage. What role does the Holy Spirit play in helping all of God's people experience the good news of the kingdom?

12. What changes would you like to see the Spirit bring into your community so that diverse people could come together?

Invite the Holy Spirit to use and to empower you to make the good news of the kingdom of God known in your church and in your community.

Now or Later
Divide a sheet of paper into two columns. In the first column, identify six people who are significantly different from you (consider race, ethnicity, culture, gender and so on). In the second column, identify a way that you could demonstrate to each—by word and deed—the message of the kingdom of God.

6

Kingdoms in Conflict

Revelation 19

Many couples struggle during their engagement. Not yet married but no longer completely single, they experience only a tantalizing foretaste of marriage's trust, commitment and intimacy. Waiting awkwardly between promise and fulfillment, an engaged couple is a metaphor for the church. As the church, we've tasted the exquisite promise of the kingdom in Jesus life, death and resurrection, yet we long for the fullness of his kingdom to come when he returns.

GROUP DISCUSSION. List ways and places it seems like evil triumphs in the world. Compose a parallel list of the ways you have seen God triumph over similar evils in Scripture. Use these two lists as the basis for prayer.

PERSONAL REFLECTION. When you think of Jesus' second coming, what images and hopes do you cherish? What do these reveal about you?

Throughout every page of Revelation, John challenges believers to trust that the King is in the process of vanquishing all opposition to his kingdom. The final chapters illustrate the fulfillment of this promise. *Read Revelation 19.*

1. How do the scenes in this passage inspire you to worship?

2. What do God's acts of judgment reveal about his character and concerns (vv. 1-5)?

Which of these traits is most important to you? Explain.

3. The multitudes in heaven praise God for his judgment against the great prostitute, which represents the corrupted political and economic systems of the world. How does your practice of worship and prayer include an awareness of evil—and God's eventual triumph over it?

4. How do your daily choices reflect a knowledge that God will judge these systems?

5. Why do many people find it difficult to thank God for judgment?

What would the universe be like if God did not judge evil?

6. The news of the wedding of the Lamb so overwhelms John that he almost worships the messenger (vv. 9-10). What about the wedding announcement of the Lamb reveals God to be praiseworthy (vv. 6-10)?

7. How is the bride prepared for this wedding in verses 7 and 8?

8. In what ways is marriage a metaphor for our relationship with Jesus?

9. Every fairytale ending involves a knight in shining armor. What about this "knight in shining armor" inspires both faithfulness and terror (vv. 11-16)?

Consider your favorite images of Jesus. How does this picture of Jesus as King of kings and Lord of lords enrich those images?

---

10. Aligned against the rider on the white horse in verses 17-20 are powerful forces: the world's political leaders, its military might and its spiritual guides. (The beast and false prophet represent satanic imitations of Jesus and the Holy Spirit.) Why would the details of this gory wedding banquet be good news to the Bride?

---

11. How should Jesus' ultimate triumph over the powers of this world —economic, political, military, spiritual—shape your daily decision making?

your church or fellowship's activities?

---

12. How does this picture of the King and his kingdom fulfill the work Jesus began during his life (which we looked at in the previous studies)?

How does this picture of Jesus' triumph compare with your hopes and dreams about Jesus' return?

Open today's newspaper and begin to ask that God's kingdom would come and his will would be done in the situations that you see described. Thank God that he will judge evil decisively.

Now or Later

Most people treat the book of Revelation as an almanac for the future. However, fundamentally, it is a worship book that invites the people of God to live wisely in light of his coming. Read through the book, and write down the advice it offers to the reader.

7

Waiting for Kingdom Come

Matthew 25:1-30

In his wise book *Waiting: Finding Hope When God Seems Silent,* Ben Patterson confesses, "I hate to wait. My image of hell is an eternity of standing in line, waiting in the lobby of some Kafkaesque bureaucracy. I write this book out of one central conviction: that at least as important as the things we wait for is the work God wants to do in us as we wait." In these three parables, Jesus instructs the disciples how to live as they wait for his kingdom to come in its fullness.

GROUP DISCUSSION. How does your workplace differ when your boss enters the room? What does this reveal about you and your coworkers?

PERSONAL REFLECTION. What's the most foolish choice you have ever made? What did you fail to consider that would have changed your choice?

Everyone struggles with the difficulty of making present-moment decisions in light of a distant future reward. We use get-rich-quick schemes, fad diets, one-night stands and CliffsNotes to replace diligent labor, intense discipline, intentional community and focused study. Faithfulness, though, is largely about delayed gratification. *Read Matthew 25:1-30.*

1. What emotions accompany the Lord's return in these two stories?

2. What emotions do you anticipate experiencing when the Lord returns? Why?

3. What characteristics and attitudes define someone who is wise in the parable (vv. 1-13)?

someone who is foolish?

4. What might be the reasons for the bridegroom's harsh response?

What does this reveal about the nature of the kingdom?

---

5. Bridesmaids had significant responsibilities in weddings. What significant responsibilities has Jesus given to his people, the church?

---

6. How have you seen your church or fellowship demonstrate foolishness or wisdom in fulfilling its kingdom responsibilities while it waits for Jesus to return?

---

7. A talent was the equivalent of several decades of wages for a common laborer. From his actions in verses 14-23, what do you learn about the master's character and values?

about his attitude toward and expectations of his servants?

---

8. Why does the unfaithful servant provoke such a harsh response from the master (vv. 24-30)?

How do you reconcile the master's empowering generosity and terrible wrath?

9. God has entrusted you with all of your opportunities, resources and experiences. Do your lifestyle choices (vocational, political, educational, social and economic) reflect the characteristics of a good servant?

Why or why not?

10. What do these parables demonstrate about what it will be like when the kingdom of God comes in its fullness?

11. Most people think of waiting as a passive experience. How could your actions during the next week demonstrate that you are actively waiting for Jesus' return?

Pray that God would enable you to be a faithful, wise servant as you wait for his return.

Now or Later

12. *Read Matthew 25:31-46.* What is the King's basis for dividing the sheep and the goats?

What does this reveal about his interests, values and priorities (vv. 31-36)?

13. Contrast responses of those on the left and on the right of the throne.

What does this reveal about their differing vision, attitudes and expectations (vv. 37-39, 44)?

14. Compare the attitudes and resulting fates of the characters in these three parables.

Track the way you spend your money and time for a week. Make one specific choice to reallocate your resources and attention to better reflect the truths of Matthew 25.

8

King of All

"Our gospel message is too small." After getting my attention with these surprising words, the conference speaker went on to say: "It has been said that God loves you and has a wonderful plan for your life, and that is true. But it is even more crucial that you understand a more foundational truth: that God loves the world and has a wonderful plan for its future."

GROUP DISCUSSION. Describe to each other your favorite ways to explain the gospel to interested non-Christians. What do they suggest about God's plans for individuals? for the world?

PERSONAL REFLECTION. Reflect on your area of study or work. What opportunities do you have to demonstrate God's love and plan for the world?

Individual lives and entire societies are changed when they encounter the good news of Jesus' life, death and resurrection. *Read Colossians 1:1-20.*

1. Identify the connections between the people mentioned in verses 3-8. What relationship does the gospel have to each of these connections?

2. What positive characteristics do you see in the people and their relationships?

3. How would our society be different if every Christian obviously demonstrated these virtues?

What external forces or personal preferences make it difficult for us to demonstrate these virtues on a daily basis?

4. According to Paul, what characteristics make up a life "worthy of the Lord" (vv. 9-12)?

5. Paul wrote to a community of believers, not to an individual. In what specific areas does your church or fellowship succeed in living a life worthy of the Lord?

fail to live a life worthy of the Lord?

6. Paul uses the metaphor of changing citizenship from the dominion of darkness to the kingdom of the Son to describe the nature of salvation in verses 12-14. Describe one specific area in which this change of allegiance has affected your lifestyle choices.

How might this change of allegiance shape your participation in your community or workplace?

7. Describe Jesus' relationship to God, all creation and the church (vv. 15-18).

8. How should what Paul teaches about Jesus help you relate to an invisible God (v. 15)?

shape your relationship with "all creation" (vv. 16-17)?

shape your relationship with the church (v. 18)?

9. What is the purpose for Christ's supremacy in all creation and the church (vv. 19-20)?

10. Christ died so that God could reconcile all things on earth to himself. In a chart, identify specific ways that (a) your community, (b) your country and (c) your culture remain unreconciled with God.

11. Besides engaging in evangelism, what concrete actions could you take to reflect God's desire for reconciliation with all things on earth?

What actions could your church or fellowship take?

Worship Jesus as the one who reigns supreme over all things, systems and structures.

Now or Later

Identify a contemporary issue or place where God's desire for reconciliation and Christ's supremacy is still not obvious, whether social (racism, war, poverty), cultural (in the arts, in the schools, in popular culture) or intellectual (relativism, anti-intellectualism, postmodernity).

Look for some resources (books, websites or people) that would help you develop an understanding and initial game plan for how to reflect God's desire for reconciliation and Christ's supremacy in these areas.

9

Living in Light of the Kingdom

We pay special attention to people's final words. A leader's last words not only provide an opportunity for the leader to reshape their legacy but also to set direction for future leaders. For example, George Washington's farewell address not only summed up his political philosophy but also created a precedent that created an unofficial term limit on the presidency that lasted until World War II.

GROUP DISCUSSION. Describe a key lesson you have learned from watching or listening to someone older than yourself.

PERSONAL REFLECTION. Imagine you had the opportunity to listen to your best friends give your eulogy. What do you think they would say about your life? What do you hope they would say?

In this letter to Timothy, Paul sums up his life and passes the torch to a younger generation of leaders. *Read 2 Timothy 3:10—4:18.*

1. Identify the types of arguments that Paul makes to encourage Timothy to stand strong in his calling.

2. What aspects of Paul's life reflect the characteristics of a person committed to the kingdom of God (3:10-14)?

How would Paul's experiences encourage Timothy to live distinctively?

3. Why does Paul have confidence in the power of Scripture to shape Timothy's life (3:15-17)?

4. Has God recently used other people or Scripture to change the way you live? How?

5. Describe a situation in which God used your life and knowledge of Scripture to transform someone else.

What could you do this week to increase your effectiveness as an agent of transformation in someone else's life?

---

6. How does Paul's final charge communicate a sense of urgency and seriousness (4:1-5)?

---

7. Do your lifestyle choices reflect a similar sense of urgency and seriousness? How?

---

8. In a chart, identify (a) the types of behavior and attitudes Paul warns Timothy he will encounter and (b) a contemporary example for each (4:3-4).

Describe someone who you think could win a hearing from these kinds of people without compromising the gospel message.

---

9. In your own words describe the source of Paul's satisfaction at his life's end (4:6-8).

What choices and decisions would help you end your life with similar contentment?

10. How do Paul's final days model his ongoing kingdom orientation (4:9-18)?

11. How does a kingdom perspective encourage you to be faithful?

Thank God for the example of older saints who have encouraged you in your faith. Ask God to use you in the life of a younger Christian to encourage them to stand firm.

Now or Later

Schedule time to read a book that will encourage you to be a faithful evangelist and teacher of Scripture. Books like Rebecca Manley Pippert's *Out of the Saltshaker* or Rick Richardson's *Evangelism Outside the Box* will encourage and enable you to be faithful witnesses to Jesus. Or consider reading a book like Gordon Fee and Douglas Stuart's *How to Read the Bible for All Its Worth* or R. C. Sproul's *Knowing Scripture* to equip you to study Scripture more faithfully.

10

Who Sits on the Throne?

Through our choices, we affirm or deny the fundamental truth of Scripture: the Lord reigns. One day every knee will bow and every tongue will confess that Jesus Christ is Lord to the glory of God the Father. Until that day arrives, however, we will struggle to keep Jesus on his rightful throne.

GROUP DISCUSSION. How would our government look different and act differently if politicians really believed that the Lord reigns?

PERSONAL REFLECTION. Review your calendar for the past month. If an objective observer reviewed the entries, what would they say you care the most about?

As the ruler of Babylon, Nebuchadnezzar ruled the dominant empire in the ancient Near East. *Read Daniel 4.*

1. What does Nebuchadnezzar seem to know about God's reign as he begins his letter (vv. 1-3)?

2. What do you learn about Nebuchadnezzar and Daniel from the way that they interact (vv. 4-27)?

3. How does Daniel model a faithful way of confronting people in authority with kingdom truths?

4. In what situation or relationship do you need to communicate biblical truth?

5. Retell Nebuchadnezzar's dream in a way that would communicate to current urban world political or business leaders (vv. 10-18).

6. Ancient people would have recognized the tree as a symbol of life and the king's role in sustaining it. Why would this dream alarm Nebuchadnezzar and Daniel?

7. Focus on verses 28-32. How do you explain the king's attitude and actions given that he has received the dream and its interpretation?

8. In what circumstances have you presumed on God's mercy and ignored his warnings?

What conditions enable you to do so?

9. The content and purpose of Nebuchadnezzar's dream are repeated three times (vv. 9-17, 20-26, 31-32). What makes this a difficult truth for people in authority to accept?

How would Daniel's suggested course of action (v. 27) demonstrate that Nebuchadnezzar understood God's warning?

10. How do the dream and its fulfillment demonstrate the ultimate authority of God's kingdom over all human structures and systems (vv. 31-33)?

11. What important truths about God does Nebuchadnezzar discover as a result of his humiliation (vv. 34-37)?

12. Why do we often learn these truths only through humiliating circumstances?

Praise the Lord for his greatness, and ask him to deal with your pride.

Now or Later

Read Daniel 1—7. Look for ways that Daniel and his friends testify to the primacy of God's kingdom in an alien and foreign culture. Notice the way God uses dreams (chapters 2 and 7), challenges to idolatry (chapters 3 and 6), and judges and rulers (chapters 4 and 5) to assert his supremacy.

Leader's Notes

MY GRACE IS SUFFICIENT FOR YOU. (2 COR 12:9)

Leading a Bible discussion can be an enjoyable and rewarding experience. But it can also be *scary*—especially if you've never done it before. If this is your feeling, you're in good company. When God asked Moses to lead the Israelites out of Egypt, he replied, "O Lord, please send someone else to do it"! (Ex 4:13). It was the same with Solomon, Jeremiah and Timothy, but God helped these people in spite of their weaknesses, and he will help you as well.

You don't need to be an expert on the Bible or a trained teacher to lead a Bible discussion. The idea behind these inductive studies is that the leader guides group members to discover for themselves what the Bible has to say. This method of learning will allow group members to remember much more of what is said than a lecture would.

These studies are designed to be led easily. As a matter of fact, the flow of questions through the passage from observation to interpretation to application is so natural that you may feel that the studies lead themselves. This study guide is also flexible. You can use it with a variety of groups— student, professional, neighborhood or church groups. Each study takes forty-five to sixty minutes in a group setting.

There are some important facts to know about group dynamics and encouraging discussion. The suggestions listed below should enable you to effectively and enjoyably fulfill your role as leader.

Preparing for the Study

1. Ask God to help you understand and apply the passage in your own life. Unless this happens, you will not be prepared to lead others. Pray too for the various members of the group. Ask God to open your hearts to the message of his Word and motivate you to action.

2. Read the introduction to the entire guide to get an overview of the entire book and the issues which will be explored.

3. As you begin each study, read and reread the assigned Bible passage to familiarize yourself with it.

4. This study guide is based on the New International Version of the Bible. It will help you and the group if you use this translation as the basis for your study and discussion.

5. Carefully work through each question in the study. Spend time in meditation and reflection as you consider how to respond.

6. Write your thoughts and responses in the space provided in the study guide. This will help you to express your understanding of the passage clearly.

7. It might help to have a Bible dictionary handy. Use it to look up any unfamiliar words, names or places. (For additional help on how to study a passage, see chapter five of *How to Lead a LifeGuide*® *Bible Study,* InterVarsity Press.)

8. Consider how you can apply the Scripture to your life. Remember that the group will follow your lead in responding to the studies. They will not go any deeper than you do.

9. Once you have finished your own study of the passage, familiarize yourself with the leader's notes for the study you are leading. These are designed to help you in several ways. First, they tell you the purpose the study guide author had in mind when writing the study. Take time to think through how the study questions work together to accomplish that purpose. Second, the notes provide you with additional background information or suggestions on group dynamics for various questions. This information can be useful when people have difficulty understanding or answering a question. Third, the leader's notes can alert you to potential problems you may encounter during the study.

10. If you wish to remind yourself of anything mentioned in the leader's notes, make a note to yourself below that question in the study.

Leading the Study

1. Begin the study on time. Open with prayer, asking God to help the group to understand and apply the passage.

2. Be sure that everyone in your group has a study guide. Encourage the group to prepare beforehand for each discussion by reading the introduction to the guide and by working through the questions in the study.

3. At the beginning of your first time together, explain that these studies are meant to be discussions, not lectures. Encourage the members of the group to participate. However, do not put pressure on those who may be hesitant to speak during the first few sessions. You may want to suggest the following guidelines to your group.

☐ Stick to the topic being discussed.

☐ Your responses should be based on the verses which are the focus of the discussion and not on outside authorities such as commentaries or speakers.

☐ These studies focus on a particular passage of Scripture. Only rarely should you refer to other portions of the Bible. This allows for everyone to participate in in-depth study on equal ground.

☐ Anything said in the group is considered confidential and will not be discussed outside the group unless specific permission is given to do so.

☐ We will listen attentively to each other and provide time for each person present to talk.

☐ We will pray for each other.

4. Have a group member read the introduction at the beginning of the discussion.

5. Every session begins with a group discussion question. The question or activity is meant to be used before the passage is read. The question introduces the theme of the study and encourages group members to begin to open up. Encourage as many members as possible to participate, and be ready to get the discussion going with your own response.

This section is designed to reveal where our thoughts or feelings need to be transformed by Scripture. That is why it is especially important not to read the passage before the discussion question is asked. The passage will tend to color the honest reactions people would otherwise give because they are, of course, supposed to think the way the Bible does.

You may want to supplement the group discussion question with an icebreaker to help people to get comfortable. See the community section of *Small Group Idea Book* for more ideas.

You also might want to use the personal reflection question with your group. Either allow a time of silence for people to respond individually or discuss it together.

6. Have a group member (or members if the passage is long) read aloud the passage to be studied. Then give people several minutes to read the passage again silently so that they can take it all in.

7. Question 1 will generally be an overview question designed to briefly survey the passage. Encourage the group to look at the whole passage, but try to avoid getting sidetracked by questions or issues that will be addressed later in the study.

8. As you ask the questions, keep in mind that they are designed to be used just as they are written. You may simply read them aloud. Or you may prefer to express them in your own words.

There may be times when it is appropriate to deviate from the study guide.

For example, a question may have already been answered. If so, move on to the next question. Or someone may raise an important question not covered in the guide. Take time to discuss it, but try to keep the group from going off on tangents.

9. Avoid answering your own questions. If necessary, repeat or rephrase them until they are clearly understood. Or point out something you read in the leader's notes to clarify the context or meaning. An eager group quickly becomes passive and silent if they think the leader will do most of the talking.

10. Don't be afraid of silence. People may need time to think about the question before formulating their answers.

11. Don't be content with just one answer. Ask, "What do the rest of you think?" or "Anything else?" until several people have given answers to the question.

12. Acknowledge all contributions. Try to be affirming whenever possible. Never reject an answer. If it is clearly off-base, ask, "Which verse led you to that conclusion?" or again, "What do the rest of you think?"

13. Don't expect every answer to be addressed to you, even though this will probably happen at first. As group members become more at ease, they will begin to truly interact with each other. This is one sign of healthy discussion.

14. Don't be afraid of controversy. It can be very stimulating. If you don't resolve an issue completely, don't be frustrated. Move on and keep it in mind for later. A subsequent study may solve the problem.

15. Periodically summarize what the group has said about the passage. This helps to draw together the various ideas mentioned and gives continuity to the study. But don't preach.

16. At the end of the Bible discussion you may want to allow group members a time of quiet to work on an idea under "Now or Later." Then discuss what you experienced. Or you may want to encourage group members to work on these ideas between meetings. Give an opportunity during the session for people to talk about what they are learning.

17. Conclude your time together with conversational prayer, adapting the prayer suggestion at the end of the study to your group. Ask for God's help in following through on the commitments you've made.

18. End on time.

Many more suggestions and helps are found in *How to Lead a LifeGuide*® *Bible Study.*

Components of Small Groups

A healthy small group should do more than study the Bible. There are four components to consider as you structure your time together.

Nurture. Small groups help us to grow in our knowledge and love of God. Bible study is the key to making this happen and is the foundation of your small group.

Community. Small groups are a great place to develop deep friendships with other Christians. Allow time for informal interaction before and after each study. Plan activities and games that will help you get to know each other. Spend time having fun together—going on a picnic or cooking dinner together.

Worship and prayer. Your study will be enhanced by spending time praising God together in prayer or song. Pray for each other's needs—and keep track of how God is answering prayer in your group. Ask God to help you to apply what you are learning in your study.

Outreach. Reaching out to others can be a practical way of applying what you are learning, and it will keep your group from becoming self-focused. Host a series of evangelistic discussions for your friends or neighbors. Clean up the yard of an elderly friend. Serve at a soup kitchen together, or spend a day working on a Habitat house.

Many more suggestions and helps in each of these areas are found in *Small Group Idea Book*. Information on building a small group can be found in *Small Group Leaders' Handbook* and *The Big Book on Small Groups* (both from Inter-Varsity Press). Reading through one of these books would be worth your time.

Study 1. The Character of the King. Psalm 145.

Purpose: To explore how God's character and nature are reflected in his kingdom.

Question 1. Notice how the psalm begins with David's personal decision to worship God the King, then highlights the generations (vv. 4-7) and concludes with the statement that all creatures will bless his holy name. Like David, we never worship alone. We stand in God's presence in the company of all of his people, stretched out in both time and space, alongside the wordless (but noticeable) worship of all of his creation.

Question 3. Notice both (a) the way one generation draws forth worship from the other and (b) how David's worship moves from personal meditation (v. 5) to public proclamation (v. 6) on God's actions and character.

Question 6. True worship always issues forth in evangelism and mission. As we recognize the glory of God in worship, we will be compelled to declare God's worth to everyone—including those who do not know yet know it. And we naturally will invite those who do not yet know God to join us in the worship of God. Evangelism and mission differ from worship only in terms of their audience. For the Israelites, true worship would have demanded action because they made no distinction between knowledge and action. One could not claim to know a truth and fail to act on that truth.

Question 8. Help the group to notice that God's kingdom agenda includes both acts of mercy and judgment. Both aspects of God's character are essential and praiseworthy. "In the Lord, justice lives alongside kindness. There is an intrinsic morality in all he does (17), and there are personal moral qualifications leading to his holy enrichments (18–20). Righteous though he is, he is also *near*, next-of-kin, to his praying people. At the same time his righteousness also looks for their sincerity (18), their reverence (19), and their love (20). His righteousness is indeed a righteousness of grace—loving, fulfilling desires, saving, watching over, but it is also the righteousness of holiness" (D. A. Carson et al., *The New Bible Commentary: 21st Century Edition* [Downers Grove, Ill.: InterVarsity Press, 1994], p. 581).

People who are oppressed and without recourse particularly celebrate that judgment will come on their behalf—if not in this life, then surely in the next. Gary Haugen, the president of the International Justice Mission, convincingly argues that for the marginalized and oppressed God's passionate condemnation of injustice is good news indeed. The group may want to read his book *Good News About Injustice* (InterVarsity Press) as a companion to this study guide. Groups of students and young adults may particularly appreciate *Good News About Injustice: Youth Edition*, which includes helpful appendices on how our vocational and educational choices can manifest God's concern for injustice, along with other helpful resources.

Study 2. The Kingdom's Coming. Mark 1:14-45.

Purpose: To discover the many areas over which Jesus' kingdom exercises authority.

Question 1. The word *kingdom* refers to the fact of God's reign, rather than to a place. Interwoven throughout the Old Testament, two strands of teaching about the kingdom of God focus on (a) the ongoing reign of God and (b) a future day when that reign will be evident to all peoples. In Jesus, both of these strands find a focus. "The great new development at the outset of the ministry of Jesus is the identifying of a point where these two can (not automatically will) be seen as the focus of life-giving tension—in Jesus himself. His ministry will demonstrate in what way God is now sovereign. The particularity of that reign will now be spelt out, in a unique way, through Jesus. It will also provide the basis on which the future reign of God will be established" (Donald English, *The Message of Mark* [Downers Grove, Ill.: InterVarsity Press, 1992], p. 50). This study demonstrates the visible extension of God's reign through the ministry of Jesus in the lives of individuals and communities through physical, spiritual and relational changes.

Questions 2-3. Changing jobs and communities create a great deal of stress— socially, emotionally and financially. (Fishing provided a secure and lucrative job in mostly agricultural Palestine.) "James and John were clearly not poor—they had 'hired servants' (v. 20), as only well-off people did (although the term could mean rented slaves, it most likely meant free hired workers). . . . This text indicates that none of these disciples left their business behind because it was going badly; they left behind well-paying jobs" (Craig Keener, *The IVP Bible Background Commentary: New Testament* [Downers Grove, Ill.: InterVarsity Press, 1993], p. 137). However, when the King calls, the disciples respond.

The early disciples' decisions also affected their families, employees and communities. Both Zebedee and Simon's mother-in-law (as well as any other family members) would have been dependent, at least in part, on the income earned by the early disciples. "Many Jewish teachers in Jesus' day felt that the greatest commandment was to honor one's parents. To abruptly leave behind one's family and the family business was a great sacrifice that went against everything the culture taught" (Keener, *Bible Background Commentary: New Testament*, p 137). In many Asian and Middle Eastern cultures today, a father's greatest fear is being abandoned by his children and left relying on hired hands. For many Asian Americans and other children of recent immigrants, this tension between filial piety and obedience to God's call defines the experience of discipleship. (For more information on this issue, read *Following Jesus Without Dishonoring Your Parents,* which explores this tension in Asian American discipleship.)

Question 4. Jesus brings religious truth and spiritual freedom to the people of Capernaum through his teaching and the exorcism of the demon. Both the possessed man and the community benefit from the exorcism. (After all, it must have been difficult worshiping with a possessed man in the synagogue!) Individuals in the group may question why Jesus prevents the demon from testifying to his identity. There may be a number of reasons: (1) the testimony of a demon would not be particularly trustworthy, (2) Jesus does not seek a compulsory testimony of his deity and (3) Mark wishes to contrast the immediate recognition of his authority by the spirit world with the slower understanding of Jesus' identity by his human disciples.

Question 5. Jesus' actions challenge authority structures and relationships that potentially stand in opposition to his kingly authority. For example, his call to the disciples challenges family loyalties and economic pragmatism; his teaching in the synagogue challenges religious tradition; his exorcism challenges the power of the kingdom of darkness; his other healing challenges the power of sickness. In all of his miracles, Jesus demonstrates the in-breaking of the kingdom of God into the sin-ravaged reality of creation. The prophets of the Old Testament looked forward to the in-breaking of the kingdom of God as a time when the peace would reign, the brokenness of creation would be healed, the effects of sin would be erased and creation would be restored to Eden-like perfection (see Is 2:1-5; 9:1-7; 11:1-9, 61).

Question 7. It might have seemed natural for Jesus to remain in Capernaum, where he had experienced success and received positive recognition for his healing ministry. Instead, after a time of solitude and prayer, Jesus insists that his ministry focus involves the proclamation of the kingdom message to those who haven't yet heard and the deliverance of those under demonic authority.

Question 9. See Leviticus 13:45-46 for more information about biblical attitudes toward leprosy (which described a number of different skin conditions, not merely Hanson's disease.) Notice the various ways (physically, emotionally, spiritually) that Jesus acts to meet the leper's holistic needs.

Question 10. It may be difficult for some in the group to identify specific commands of Christ that they may be disobeying. You might want to begin together with the practical implications of the Great Commandment (Mt 22:37-39), the Great Commission (Mt 28:16-20) or the golden rule (Mt 7:12) as a way of starting the discussion. The question's goal, however, is not to burden people with guilt; rather, it is to point the group toward faithful obedience that will benefit those whom Christ intends to bless through his people.

Study 3. An Offer You Can't Ignore. Matthew 13:1-45.

Purpose: To explore the different responses to the kingdom message of Jesus.

Background. Jesus often used parables as an extended metaphor about the nature and values of his kingdom. Though parables may contain allegorical elements, parables primarily attempt to communicate one or two key truths. Therefore, do not necessarily expect a one-to-one correspondence between the objects or people in a parable and its interpretation. Allow the context of the parable (the questions raised just prior to the story or Jesus' own introduction to the parable) to determine the parable's meaning. David Wenham's *The Parables of Jesus* provides a well-informed and readable guide to the parables.

Question 1. Encourage the group to be creative in adapting the parable to life today while remaining faithful to the intention of the text. Being asked to transpose the parable into a different context will challenge the group to observe details more closely and to focus on faithfully interpreting the text's meaning.

Question 2. Jesus gives the secret of the kingdom to those who come to him and pursue an answer. He withholds the secret of the kingdom from those who fail to come and pursue him. The difference? Those who come demonstrate personal engagement with what they hear and personal commitment to understand and express what they know. "Thus prospective disciples have a measure of choice: only those who press into his inner circle, those who persevere to mature discipleship, will prove to be good soil. . . . Only those who press close to Jesus, persevering until they understand the real point of his teaching, will prove to be long-term disciples" (Craig Keener, *Matthew* [Downers Grove, Ill.: InterVarsity Press, 1997], pp. 236, 41). Those who hear, but fail to respond to what they know, remain ignorant. This is a challenging word to those whose knowledge far outstrips their obedience.

Question 4. The parable of the weeds focuses on the currently intermixed nature of the kingdom of God and the children of darkness. Jesus uses a familiar agricultural experience to focus the listeners' attention. "The most basic staple of the Palestinian diet (and the ancient diet in general) was bread; thus wheat was critical. But a poisonous weed, a kind of ryegrass known as darnel (usually translated *tares*) looked like wheat in the early stages and could only be distinguished from it when the ear appeared" (Keener, *IVP Bible Background Commentary: New Testament*, p. 83). The parable reminds us of the need to remain cautious and humble in our judgments and confident and bold in God's ultimate execution of justice.

Question 6. You may need to help the group consider ways Christians with kingdom values have changed society. Notable examples in the area of racial justice and ethnic reconciliation might include William Wilberforce (who spent over forty years working to eliminate the slave trade in the British Empire), abolitionists in the United States and key individuals in the Civil Rights movement. Other examples might include Lord Shaftesbury, who led the crusade for child labor laws and other key social reforms in Great Britain, the work of missionaries to India who led the work to abolish the practice of burning widows alive, the influence of World Vision or the International Justice Mission on the oppressed of the world. Christian intellectuals also have had significant influence on several fields, including academic philosophy and practical linguistics.

Question 7. Darnel and wheat were indistinguishable until the wheat had demonstrated its fruitfulness. "The fields were normally weeded in the spring, but if the weeds were discovered too late—as here—one would risk uprooting the wheat with them; the master does not want to risk his wheat. Once they were fully grown, however, harvesters could cut the wheat just below the head, leaving the shorter tares to be cut separately" (Keener, *IVP Bible Background Commentary: New Testament,* p. 83). Help the group to consider the relationship between bearing fruit and demonstrating our citizenship in the kingdom of God.

Question 11. In war-torn Palestine, people often buried their treasures for safekeeping. If the treasure was not reclaimed, the owner of the land on which the treasure was buried became the owner of the treasure. "Jesus lays the entire emphasis on the price the man is ready to pay to invest in this treasure far greater than any he already owns. Although this treasure, like the kingdom, is hidden to most of the world, not only does the man recognize that its value outweighs all he has, but (unlike most of us today) he acts accordingly" (Keener, *Matthew,* p. 246).

The final two parables focus on the incalculable value of the kingdom of God. "True, the kingdom is available to us only by grace through faith; but genuine faith means genuinely embracing and yielding to God's reign, not simply acknowledging it and then passing it by as if it did not exist. The kingdom is a treasure, and those who really believe it will sacrifice everything else in their lives for its agendas" (Keener, *Matthew,* p. 245).

Study 4. Mission Statement for a Kingdom. Matthew 20:1-28.

Purpose: To explore the kingdom values taught and demonstrated by Jesus.

Question 3. We value equality, while Jesus' kingdom values prioritize grace. "In a society with no welfare provision or trade unions, where unemployment meant starvation, the action of the *landowner* in employing extra workers whom he did not really need so late in the day was an act of generosity. But even more extraordinary was the rate of pay, which made no economic sense, and understandably provoked grumbling among those who felt unfairly treated. It was not *unfair,* of course. No-one was underpaid; it was just that some were treated with 'unreasonable' generosity. That is what the kingdom of heaven is like. God's grace is not limited by our ideas of fairness; his gifts are far beyond what we can deserve. But, like the elder brother in the story of the Prodigal Son, we find it hard to abandon our human scale of values (especially when comparing ourselves with others!) and to accept the large-heartedness of God towards those we regard as undeserving" (*New Bible Commentary,* p. 930).

Question 4. Though some commentators suggest that this parable should not be extended beyond the spiritual realm, it seems unusual that we desire an economy of grace in the spiritual world but an economy of merit in our daily lives. Push the group to consider what their world would be like if Christians acted with an economy of grace in government, work, family and neighborhood.

Question 5. Verses 17-19 illustrate the truth of Jesus' teaching in verse 16: the first shall be last. The verses contain Jesus' third announcement of his suffering and death in Matthew, and they clearly indicate that the way to greatness is the way of the cross, a way which includes self-sacrifice, suffering, sin-bearing and sorrow. "The effect is to emphasize not only the totality of the rejection (Jewish leaders and Gentiles), but also the humiliation and the harrowing pain; this is to be no glorious martyrdom, but an ugly, sordid butchery" (R. T. France, *Matthew* [Grand Rapids, Mich.: Eerdmans, 1985], p. 291). In contrast, the mother of Zebedee's sons seems to imagine the coming of a glorious kingdom in which her sons can enjoy prominence.

Question 13. Craig Keener points out that the borrowing of the donkey reminds us "Jesus as Lord has the right to whatever his followers claim to own." He continues, "The donkey's owner probably saw it as helpful hospitality to visitors to the feast or perhaps as the honor of helping on his way a famous rabbi. . . . The text is messianic, as ancient interpreters generally acknowledged, but applying this part to himself redefines Jesus' messiahship: officials used donkeys for civil, not military, processions (e.g., 1 Kings 1:33). Thus this text is not a 'triumphal entry' in the sense of Roman triumphal processions; it is Jerusalem's reception of a meek and peaceful king" (*IVP Bible Background Commentary: New Testament,* p. 100). However, Zechariah 9, which Jesus refers to in Matthew 21:5, speaks of a king who brings not peace but judgment. (Another parallel exists between Jesus and Jehu, who entered the city on cloaks and who subsequently slaughtered the evil house of Ahab. See 2 Kings 9:13 and the chapters that follow.)

Study 5. Kingdom in Word and Deeds. Acts 8:4-25.

Purpose: To investigate the role of the Holy Spirit in proclaiming and uniting the kingdom of God.

Question 1. The enmity and mutual prejudice between Samaritans and Jews developed from a mix of ethnocentrism, religious pride, political tension and historical violence. Jews despised the Samaritans, who were the biracial descendants of Jews who had intermarried with Gentiles during the Assyrian occupation of Israel (2 Kings 17:24-41). The Samaritans returned the feeling.

During intertestamental times, each group attacked the other group's primary place of worship. The historian Josephus recounts that the Jews attacked Mount Gerizim and the Samaritans attacked the temple in Jerusalem. The shocking power of the parable of the Good Samaritan (Lk 10:25-37) and the account of Jesus' interaction with the Samaritan woman (Jn 4:1-42) assume this background. This background also explains why James and John ask Jesus if they can call down fire on Samaritans who refuse to heed Jesus' message (Lk 9:51-56). Both Philip and the Samaritans would have mutual prejudices, suspicions and fears that were well founded given the history between their peoples.

Question 2. This question may be difficult for people to answer because they may worry about sounding racist, prejudiced, provincial or small-minded. Be prepared to share honestly about your own current prejudices and fears. Ajith Fernando writes, "While it is true that we live in a global village, there is much animosity between the peoples of different nations and groups—north versus south, rich versus poor, Western versus non-Western, American versus British, black versus white, Jew versus Arab, one ethnic group versus another ethnic group, hierarchical versus egalitarian; these are all divisions we face in the world, and they may have entered into the life of the church as well. A person may aggravate the problem by denying that there is a problem, which sends a message to the other party that this person is insensitive to their feelings" (*Acts* [Grand Rapids, Mich.: Zondervan, 1998], p. 279). If the group gets stuck, rephrase the question: "Historically, what groups of people had similar fears or prejudices toward each other?"

Question 4. Throughout the book of Acts, miraculous gifts validate the content and advance of the gospel message. A great deal of controversy exists about the validity and meaning of similar spiritual gifts today. Though this is an important discussion, do not let the group get distracted from the primary focus of the chapter on the way the message of the gospel crosses ethnic lines. (The Jews did not consider the Samaritans to be Gentiles, but neither did they consider them to be Jews.) Notice the similarities between Philip's initial ministry and Jesus' initial ministry which we observed in the study of Mark 1:14-45.

Question 5. Too often when the church speaks on the "unity of the body of Christ" or the "multiethnic reality of the kingdom," its deeds fail to illustrate the truth of its words. A series of emotional hugs and confessions in a stadium do not make for true unity or reconciliation. For a powerful indictment of the evangelical church's failure to address racial enmity, read Michael O. Emerson and Christian Smith, *Divided by Faith* (New York: Oxford University Press, 2000). For a brutally honest but hope-filled counterpoint, read Spencer

Perkins and Chris Rice, *More Than Equals: Racial Healing for the Sake of the Gospel*, rev. ed. (Downers Grove, Ill.: InterVarsity Press, 2000).

Question 9. This passage serves as a critical passage for Christians who debate whether or not all true believers experience a second-stage "baptism of the Holy Spirit." Encourage the group not to be distracted by this otherwise important question but to focus on the role of this story in the Acts narrative. Throughout the book of Acts, as the gospel crosses historically inviolable ethnic lines, the Holy Spirit clearly manifests himself in ways which the Jewish apostles in Jerusalem cannot deny. In the earlier chapters of the book, the church had witnessed the meaning of Jesus' life, death and resurrection in Jerusalem. Philip's mission to Samaria represents the next stage of the fulfillment of Jesus' command to the disciples, "But you will receive power when the Holy Spirit comes on you; and you will be my witnesses in Jerusalem, and in all Judea and Samaria, and to the ends of the earth" (Acts 1:8). (This verse provides the outline of the book of Acts.) As a result of Philip's faithful ministry, the Samaritans come to faith in Jesus, much to the apparent shock of the Jerusalem apostles who immediately send Peter and John to Samaria. And, once they arrive, the Holy Spirit comes.

See also, for example, Peter's testimony about the conversion of the first Gentile believer, Cornelius (Acts 10:44-48; 11:15-17), which involves a similarly distinctive manifestation by the Holy Spirit. Notice, also, how Peter uses this manifestation of the Holy Spirit as a way of convincing the more conservative Jewish Christians to welcome Gentile believers as full members of the church (Acts 15:6-11).

Study 6. Kingdoms in Conflict. Revelation 19.

Purpose: To discover how Jesus' kingdom overcomes all rival kingdoms.

Background. The book of Revelation can be difficult to interpret and frightening (or unhelpfully fascinating) to many people. Terrifying and incomprehensible images, strange and oddly systematic numbered symbols, and cataclysmic but ultimately redemptive judgments flash across the page. When leading a group in a single chapter of Revelation, it may be most helpful to remember that the chief concern of apocalyptic writers (like the author of Revelation) is to challenge readers to worship and to remain faithful until God vindicates his people, renews his broken creation and decisively triumphs over evil. The key theme: God is in control of history and will triumph. For a helpful description of how to interpret apocalyptic literature, see the chapter in Gordon Fee and Douglas Stuart's *How to Read the Bible for All Its Worth*, 2nd ed. (Grand Rapids, Mich.: Zondervan, 1993).

Question 2. Help the group to see how the heavenly multitude relates judgment to many of God's attributes that we generally think of as positive: salvation, glory, power, holiness, redemption and so on. God's judgment against evil and the forces of oppression is an expression of his holy love and passionate commitment to his people and his purposes. In fact, full salvation must include the elimination of evil.

Question 3. If the group has time, quickly review the image of the prostitute in chapters 17 and 18. Encourage the group to focus on the big-picture impression left by the imagery, rather than getting bogged down in attempting to identify every detail. Though theological systems shape the interpretation of the image in different ways, almost all of them agree that the prostitute represents a figure who enjoys incredible wealth (17:4), revels in sin (17:5), persecutes the church (17:6), controls political systems (17:9-12, 15; 18:3), deals in luxuries and slaves (18:11-13) and benefits from commercial relationships (18:15-19).

Question 5. Modern people often dichotomize God's love and God's judgment. Scripture, however, holds these attributes in creative tension by demonstrating that God's judgment reflects his implacable wrath toward sin as an expression of his deep covenant love. Humanity, in deep denial over the reality of our sin, cannot imagine God would be angered by our treachery and rebellion. However, a God who did not judge evil would be complicit with it —and a horror beyond imagining. An amoral, omnipotent being with no commitment to truth, righteousness or holiness would be unable to distinguish between good and evil, truth and falsity. While we would like to worship only a God of sweetness and light, Scripture reminds us that light reveals our sin.

Question 7. Help group members notice the interplay between the bride making herself ready (active voice) and being given fine linen which represents the righteous acts of the saints (passive voice). The bride makes herself ready by doing the righteous acts that were given her to do—demonstrating a wonderful interplay between our actions and God's grace. Paul highlights this same truth in Ephesians 2:10, "For we are God's workmanship, created in Christ Jesus to do good works, which God prepared in advance for us to do."

Question 8. Marriage provides a number of parallels in terms of total intimacy, absolute trust and unwavering commitment with our eventual relationship with Jesus.

Question 10. This question (along with question 5) requires some sensitivity on the part of the leader. Small group members with unsaved members of their family often (and rightly) struggle with the reality of God's judgment. Others will be troubled with God's ability to inflict judgment so broadly. Encourage the group to reflect on what they see of God's character in the prior verses that may give them perspective on the nature of God's judgment ("true and just," v. 2). Just as the text directs us to God's mercy and justice, it also reminds us that we should not pronounce judgment ourselves. That task is left to God alone.

Study 7. Waiting for Kingdom Come. Matthew 25:1-30.

Purpose: To consider the ways Jesus expects us to be faithful until the kingdom comes fully.

Question 1. In the prior chapters of Matthew, Jesus has been instructing his disciples on his eventual return to bring the kingdom in its fullness. Beginning in chapter 25, he tells them how to live until he returns. The emotional focus of the following parables is on anticipation and faithful obedience.

Question 3. Throughout Scripture, wisdom "is intensely practical, not theoretical. Basically, wisdom is the art of being successful, of forming the correct plan to gain the desired results. . . . Wisdom takes insights gleaned from the knowledge of God's ways and applies them in the daily walk. This combination of insight and obedience (and all insight must issue in obedience) relates wisdom to the prophetic emphasis on the knowledge (i.e., the cordial love and obedience) of God" (I. Howard Marshall et al., eds., *The New Bible Dictionary* [Downers Grove, Ill.: InterVarsity Press, 1996], p. 1244).

In biblical times, bridesmaids were responsible to escort the groom to the bride's family home. From there, they would accompany the entire bridal party to the groom's house for the wedding ceremony, which was held in the evening. Help the group consider not only the wise virgins' practical preparations but also their single-minded focus on being ready when the groom arrives. They demonstrate wisdom by understanding their role, the situation and their duties. The foolish virgins do not.

The lamps carried by the virgins were most likely torches—sticks wrapped with oil-soaked rags. They would have burned for only fifteen minutes before new oil-soaked rags would need to be applied (Keener, *IVP Bible Background Commentary: New Testament*, p. 116).

Question 4. People in your group may struggle with the bridegroom's absolute, harsh response to the foolish bridesmaids. The bridegroom demonstrates not only the importance he places on the wedding but also the importance he places on the bridesmaids' responsibilities. He treats them as morally responsible agents who have been entrusted with a significant responsibility. Keener provides some perspective: "Being a bridesmaid was a great honor; to be insultingly unprepared and shut out of the feast was the stuff of which young women's nightmares were made. . . . The foolish brides-maids missed the entire procession back to the groom's house, along with the festive singing and dancing. They also missed the critical element of the Jew-ish wedding, in which the bride was brought into the groom's home under the wedding canopy. Having insulted the dignity of the host, they were not admitted to the feast, which lasted for seven days following the ceremony" (*IVP Bible Background Commentary: New Testament*, pp. 116-17). Though some in the group may wonder if the passage speaks to the issue of eternal se-curity, the key point of the parable is being prepared for Jesus' return.

Question 7. The master entrusts his servants with immense wealth and then departs. This suggests he trusts his servants with significant responsibility, expects faithful activity in his absence and anticipates results. Upon his re-turn, he expresses praise and offers generous rewards in response to their ini-tiative. This master ennobles his servants with dignity and respect by treating them as morally responsible, vocationally competent agents of his estate, rather than as mindless automatons.

Question 8. Commentators disagree on why the master responds so harshly to the unfaithful servant. More squeamish commentators suggest that the master sarcastically mimics the servant's unflattering description of the mas-ter's character and ironically acts in the way that the unfaithful servant ex-pects: "So you thought I was a hard man, did you? I'll show you hard!"

Other commentators, more comfortable with the master's anger, suggest that the unfaithful servant's failure both to understand his master's character and to undertake his responsibilities faithfully properly rouses the master's wrath. The second interpretation seems more consistent with the bride-groom's actions in the prior parable (and the Son of Man's actions in the para-ble that follows). The master offers the servants the dignity of stewarding his estate and representing his interests, and his immense wrath is proportional to the immense value of the ennobling offer the unfaithful servant rejects.

Group members may struggle with any suggestion that God may be simi-larly harsh in his evaluation of our faithfulness—or the faithlessness of oth-ers. While it is true that we are saved by grace and contribute nothing to our own salvation, these kingdom parables clearly teach that we will be evaluated by God in light of our faithful initiative in completing the good works for which he saved us (Eph 2:10). We cannot reduce the gospel to cheap grace.

Question 10. When Jesus returns, his people will rejoice and his enemies will mourn. Though every knee will bow and every tongue confess that Jesus Christ is Lord to the glory of God the Father, many will do so in shock, horror and de-spair as they recognize that what they have denied their entire lives is, in fact,

true. When he announced his kingdom, Jesus offered forgiveness, pardon and
redemption. When he consummates his kingdom, he will execute judgment.

Question 12. Jesus specifically identifies the hungry, thirsty, alien, naked,
sick and prisoners as members of his family (that is, his disciples). (Some
members of the group may be troubled that Jesus seems to be concerned only
with his disciples in this parable.) Jesus expects that true disciples will share
and demonstrate a similar holistic (but unselfconscious) concern for the
physical, emotional and social well-being of fellow believers.

The parable also sharply rebukes anyone who would understand the kingdom of God in merely spiritual terms or reduce it to a personal relationship
with Jesus. The King assesses the loyalty of his citizens not by pledges of allegiance (calling on him as Lord) but by their down-to-earth manifestation of
his kingdom's values, priorities and concerns.

Study 8. King of All. Colossians 1:1-20.

Purpose: To understand that Jesus' kingdom extends over the cosmos because
of who he is and what he has accomplished.

Group discussion. Some people in the group may struggle to remember a gospel outline; therefore, bring a few gospel presentations that people can review.
Several popular gospel outlines: "Circles of Belonging" (available at www.inter-
varsity.org/witness/), "The Four Spiritual Laws" (available at www.fourspiritual-
laws.org) or the "Bridge Diagram" (available at www.navigators.org under
"Resources"). As you discuss the diagrams, pay attention to the way they describe
humanity's problem and God's purpose for our salvation.

Question 1. All of the people mentioned in this section are linked by their response to the gospel: Epaphras brought the gospel to Colosse, and the Colossians responded to it with faith in Jesus and love for all the saints—provoking
Paul's prayers of thanksgiving—which is the same way that people around
the world are responding to the gospel.

Question 2. In these five verses, Paul weaves a complex tapestry of faith,
hope and love. The Colossians demonstrate faith in Jesus, and the body of
Christ receives their love as a result of the Colossians' hope in the truth of the
gospel. This same hope-filled gospel flourishes in the lives of people around
the world in the same way it has flourished in this local body of believers.
Their faith, hope and love reflect the faith-filled evangelistic ministry of Epaphras and inspire Paul's thanksgiving and worship.

Question 4. Help the group to notice not only how people become equipped
to live lives worthy of the Lord (v. 9) but also how their lives should be different as a result (vv. 10-12).

Question 6. Changing citizenship involves more than a change of passports. It requires an absolute change of loyalties, a wholehearted commitment to advance and defend the new country's interests, and a thoroughgoing decision to submit to its authority. For example, all people wishing to become citizens of the United States swear:

> I hereby declare, on oath, that I absolutely and entirely renounce and abjure all allegiance and fidelity to any foreign prince, potentate, state, or sovereignty of whom or which I have heretofore been a subject or citizen; that I will support and defend the Constitution and laws of the United States of America against all enemies, foreign and domestic; that I will bear true faith and allegiance to the same; that I will bear arms on behalf of the United States when required by the law; that I will perform noncombatant service in the Armed Forces of the United States when required by the law; that I will perform work of national importance under civilian direction when required by the law; and that I take this obligation freely without any mental reservation or purpose of evasion; so help me God.

Paul suggests that this same total change in loyalty, commitment and service takes place in the process of our salvation.

Question 7. Some in the group may be confused by the phrase, "the first-born over all creation." Jehovah's Witnesses, among other groups, use this verse to suggest Jesus was created and not God. However, "in the OT 'first-born' occurs 130 times to describe one who is supreme or first in time. It also refers to one who had a special place in the father's love: so 'Israel is my first-born son' (Ex. 4:22). Although 'firstborn' can speak of one who is the first in a series (cf. v 18; Rom. 8:29), this cannot be its significance here; the context makes it plain that Jesus is not the first of all created beings for ('because') he is the one by whom the whole creation came into being (16). Unfortunately the English word 'firstborn' does not draw attention to this notion of supremacy or priority of rank. As the *firstborn* Christ is unique, being distinguished from all creation (cf. Heb. 1:6). He is both prior to and supreme over that creation since he is its Lord. . . .

"The whole of creation is established permanently in him alone. He is the sustainer of the universe and the unifying principle of its life. Apart from his *continuous* sustaining activity (indicated by the tense of the Greek verb) all would fall apart (cf. Heb. 1:2–3)" (*New Bible Commentary*, pp. 1266-67). He is also the head of the church. As a result, Jesus reigns over both the original creation and the redeemed creation, the natural and the supernatural.

Question 8. If in Christ all things hold together and he is preeminent in all creation, we must affirm his lordship over every aspect of creation. At the founding of the Free University of Amsterdam, Abraham Kuyper, a Dutch theologian, politician and journalist, proclaimed, "There is not one square inch in the whole of human endeavor over which Christ, who is Lord over all, does not cry out, 'This is mine! This belongs to me!'" In part, this demands that we acknowledge that all truth is God's truth, that we repent of dividing the world into secular and sacred categories, and that we work to press in kingdom values and biblical truth into the everyday activities of our world. This needs to be done not by quoting Bible verses incessantly but by developing a Christian worldview and a philosophy of cultural engagement that are marked by the cross as a model of self-sacrifice, humility, grace and holiness. For practical help in developing a Christian worldview, read James W. Sire, *The Discipleship of the Mind: Learning to Love God in the Ways We Think* (Downers Grove, Ill.: InterVarsity Press, 1990).

If Christ is preeminent in the church, we must affirm his sovereign control over our church's life and demonstrate appropriate humility in its triumphs.

Question 9. This text ends by pointing to how all things will be reconciled through Christ's death.

> The opening words of the paragraph had stated that all things had been created in, through and for Christ. He is their Lord in creation. What is not spelled out, however, is what has happened to all things *since* creation: the unity and harmony of the cosmos have suffered a serious breach, needing reconciliation (*cf.* Gn. 3). It was God's good pleasure to *reconcile all things* through Christ (2 Cor. 5:19). Heaven and earth have been brought back to the order for which God made them. The universe is under its Lord, and cosmic peace has been restored. Reconciliation and *making peace* (which includes the idea of pacification, *i.e.* over-throwing evil) are used synonymously to describe the mighty work which Christ achieved in history through his death *on the cross* as a sacrifice (Rom. 3:25; 1 Cor. 11:25; Eph. 1:7). The *peace* which Christ has brought may be 'freely accepted, or . . . compulsorily imposed' (F. F. Bruce). . . . Although all things will *finally* unite to bow in the name of Jesus and to acknowledge him as Lord (Phil. 2:10–11), it is not to be supposed that this will be done gladly by all, and to suggest that v 20 points to a universal reconciliation in which every person will finally enjoy the blessings of salvation is unwarranted." (*New Bible Commentary,* p. 1267)

Study 9. Living in Light of the Kingdom. 2 Timothy 3:10—4:18.

Purpose: To understand life and ministry in light of Christ's kingdom and return.

Question 1. This question invites the group to take a big-picture look at Paul's argument and pushes the group to identify the various ways Paul attempts to encourage and equip Timothy. Help the group observe that Paul (a) reminds Timothy of the examples of faithfulness that he has observed (3:10-15); (b) affirms Timothy's experience of Scripture's power (3:15-17); (c) exhorts Timothy to minister faithfully in unfaithful times (4:1-5); (d) asserts that his own ministry is ending (4:6-8); and (e) models what kingdom-minded ministry looks like (4:9-18).

Question 2. "One might paraphrase the apostle's double exhortation to Timothy in verses 10 to 14 like this: 'But as for you, in spite of all the current false teaching, what you have been closely following is *my* doctrine and *my* way of life, together with *my* purpose, faith, patience, love, endurance, persecution and sufferings. . . . Wicked men and charlatans, deceiving others and themselves deceived, will still make their strange progress from bad to worse. But as for you, you are not to progress in any direction least of all away from or beyond my teaching (for that would be declension, not advance). On the contrary, you are to stand firm, to continue and abide in what you learned and have believed, because you know from whom you learned it" (John R. W. Stott, *The Message of 2 Timothy* [Downers Grove, Ill.: InterVarsity Press, 1973], pp. 92-93).

Question 6. By invoking the Lord's presence, Christ's return and judgment, and his kingdom coming, Paul underlines the gravity of his charge to Timothy—as well as the eternal significance of his work and the significant consequences of unfaithfulness. "Both those who preach the word and those who listen to it must give an account to Christ when he appears" (Stott, *Message of 2 Timothy,* p. 110).

Question 9. Even though the work in Ephesus, where Timothy was based, struggled, Paul looks back on his ministry with the contentment of a faithful worker. "He has fought the good fight, finished the race and kept the faith. His lifeblood is on the point of being poured out. His little boat is about to set sail. He is eagerly awaiting his crown. These facts are to be Timothy's third spur to faithfulness. . . . So then, in view of the coming of Christ to judgment, of the contemporary world's distaste for the gospel and of the imprisoned apostle's imminent death, the latter's charge to Timothy had a solemn urgency: *Preach the word!*" (Stott, *Message of 2 Timothy,* pp. 115-16).

Question 10. Help the group to notice Paul's desire for the community of believers, his continued focus on doing ministry, his commitment to studying Scripture, his experience of persecution, his experience of the Lord's presence and empowerment, his confidence in the kingdom's triumph, and his expectation of vindication. Paul does not anticipate a quiet retirement filled with rest and relaxation. Rather, he is committed to spending his final days in the same way that he invested his active ministry: doing the very things that he exhorts Timothy to do.

Study 10. Who Sits on the Throne? Daniel 4.

Purpose: To learn how God reigns over the nations.

Question 2. Help the group to see Nebuchadnezzar's deep respect for and trust in Daniel, even if he misunderstands the source of Daniel's gifts and abilities. Also help them notice Daniel's genuine loyalty, deep respect and faithful truth-telling to this pagan king. In combination, grace and truth build bridges in difficult conversations. Successful prophetic speakers know that you cannot change people you hate.

Question 4. It will be easy for group members to focus on "popular" moral issues where the church has a negative word of rebuke or condemnation. However, also encourage them to consider places, relationships and situations where a positive biblical truth needs to be said. For example, it's easy to condemn sexual immorality; it is much more difficult (but perhaps more redemptive) to affirm our belief in the dignity of all people as created in God's image, the positive delight of sexual intimacy within the boundaries of a permanent, heterosexual marriage relationship, and the affirmation of our universal need for interpersonal intimacy, commitment and trust.

Question 5. The dreams draw on a popular motif in the mostly agrarian ancient Near East. "The concept of the cosmic tree in the center of the world is a common motif in the ancient Near East. It is also used in Ezekiel 31. The roots of the tree are fed by the great subterranean ocean, and its top merges with the clouds, thus binding together the heavens, the earth and the netherworld" (John Walton et al., *The IVP Bible Background Commentary: Old Testament* [Downers Grove, Ill.: InterVarsity Press, 2000], p. 736). The tree represents the fruitfulness and flourishing of life represented by the king.

In contrast, urban dwellers today do not think of trees as symbols of strength, power or majesty. Encourage the group to consider symbols from commerce (such as buildings or corporate logos), government (military or legislative icons) or the academy (university mascots or computer systems) which represent those values to city dwellers.

Question 6. In Scripture cutting down a tree is seen as a symbol of judgment.

"This judgment is applied at a corporate national level as well as at an individual level, and the imagery of the tree applies here also. Pharaoh, king of Egypt, and his hordes are represented by the cedar of Lebanon (Ezek 31) that the Lord cast down. Nebuchadnezzar's kingdom is to be cut down, signified by the tree that is to be hewn down but left with its stump in the ground, indicating the hope of possible restoration (Dan 4)" (Leland Ryken et al., *Dictionary of Biblical Imagery* [Downers Grove, Ill.: InterVarsity Press, 2000], p. 891). Jesus uses a similar illustration to describe the kingdom of God in Mark 4:30-32.

Question 7. Nebuchadnezzar lives in a world of privilege, power and comfort. It is easy to ignore warnings of judgment when nothing else in life indicates that judgment is imminent.

Question 9. Daniel challenges Nebuchadnezzar to demonstrate his repentance by acting justly and demonstrating mercy. Both qualities reflect the character of God and the nature of his kingly reign. Nebuchadnezzar must recognize that God's holy and merciful rule requires both a change of heart (personal holiness) and a commitment to action (systemic action on behalf of the oppressed).

Greg Jao serves InterVarsity Christian Fellowship/USA as associate general counsel and divisional director for northern Illinois/northwest Indiana. He is a contributing author to Following Jesus Without Dishonoring Your Parents, *a discipleship book for Asian Americans.*

What Should We Study Next?

A good place to continue your study of Scripture would be with a book study. Many groups begin with a Gospel such as *Mark* (20 studies by Jim Hoover) or *John* (26 studies by Douglas Connelly). These guides are divided into two parts so that if twenty or twenty-six weeks seems like too much to do at once, the group can feel free to do half and take a break with another topic. Later you might want to come back to it. You might prefer to try a shorter letter. *Philippians* (9 studies by Donald Baker), *Ephesians* (11 studies by Andrew T. and Phyllis J. Le Peau) and *1 & 2 Timothy and Titus* (11 studies by Pete Sommer) are good options. If you want to vary your reading with an Old Testament book, consider *Ecclesiastes* (12 studies by Bill and Teresa Syrios) for a challenging and exciting study.

There are a number of interesting topical LifeGuide studies as well. Here are some options for filling three or four quarters of a year:

Basic Discipleship
Christian Beliefs, 12 studies by Stephen D. Eyre
Christian Character, 12 studies by Andrea Sterk & Peter Scazzero
Christian Disciplines, 12 studies by Andrea Sterk & Peter Scazzero
Evangelism, 12 studies by Rebecca Pippert & Ruth Siemens

Building Community
Fruit of the Spirit, 9 studies by Hazel Offner
Spiritual Gifts, 12 studies by Charles & Anne Hummel
Christian Community, 10 studies by Rob Suggs

Character Studies
David, 12 studies by Jack Kuhatschek
New Testament Characters, 10 studies by Carolyn Nystrom
Old Testament Characters, 12 studies by Peter Scazzero
Women of the Old Testament, 12 studies by Gladys Hunt

The Trinity
Meeting God, 12 studies by J. I. Packer
Meeting Jesus, 13 studies by Leighton Ford
Meeting the Spirit, 10 studies by Douglas Connelly